THE AFRICAN AMERICAN
EXPERIENCE
FROM SLAVERY TO THE PRESIDENCY

BARACK OBAMA
AND THE IDEA OF A
POSTRACIAL SOCIETY

EDITED BY
ZOE LOWERY

Britannica®
Educational Publishing

IN ASSOCIATION WITH
MATTESON PUBLIC LIBRARY
ROSEN
EDUCATIONAL SERVICES

Published in 2016 by Britannica Educational Publishing (a trademark of Encyclopædia Britannica, Inc.) in association with The Rosen Publishing Group, Inc.
29 East 21st Street, New York, NY 10010

Distributed exclusively by Rosen Publishing.
To see additional Britannica Educational Publishing titles, go to rosenpublishing.com.

First Edition

Britannica Educational Publishing
J. E. Luebering: Director, Core Reference Group
Anthony L. Green: Editor, Compton's by Britannica

Rosen Publishing
Hope Lourie Killcoyne: Executive Editor
Zoe Lowery: Editor
Nelson Sá: Art Director
Brian Garvey: Designer
Cindy Reiman: Photography Manager
Introduction and supplementary material by Meredith Day.

Library of Congress Cataloging-in-Publication Data

Barack Obama and the idea of a postracial society/edited by Zoe Lowery.—First edition.
    pages cm. — (The African American experience: from slavery to the presidency)
Includes bibliographical references and index.
ISBN 978-1-68048-051-1 (library bound)
1. African Americans—Social conditions—21st century—Juvenile literature. 2. United States—Race relations—Juvenile literature. 3. Racism—United States—Juvenile literature. 4. Obama, Barack—Influence—Juvenile literature. I. Lowery, Zoe.
E185.86.B36 2015
305.896'0730905—dc23

2014042501

Manufactured in the United States of America

Photo credits: Cover (Obama) Mark Makela/Getty Images; cover (background) Caiaimage/Robert Daly/OJO+/Getty Images; p. 5 MSgt Cecilio Ricardo, U.S. Air Force/U.S. Department of Defense; p. 9 Encyclopædia Britannica, Inc.; pp. 12-13 Jeanne Louise Bulliard—Lions Gate/The Kobal Collection; p. 14 Francois Durand/Getty Images Entertainment/Thinkstock; pp. 17, 56 © AP Images; p. 19 Scott Gries/Getty Images; p. 21 Bongarts/Getty Images; pp. 24-25 Walter Sanders/The Life Picture Collection/Getty Images; pp. 26–27 The Life Picture Collection/Getty Images; p. 29 Pool/Getty Images; p. 30 Francis Miller/The Life Picture Collection/Getty Images; pp. 32–33 Bloomberg/Getty Images; p. 35 AP Images/Obama for America; p. 37 New York Daily News/Getty Images; p. 39 Scott Olson/Getty Images; pp. 40–41 Emmanuel Dunand/AFP/Getty Images; pp. 42–43, 46–47, 49 Official White House photo by Pete Souza; p. 52 Afro American Newspapers/Gado/Archive Photos/Getty Images; p. 54 The Washington Post/Getty Images; pp. 58–59 Thomas Koehler/Photothek/Getty Images; pp. 60–61 Tim Boyle/Getty Images; p. 62 Photo Researchers/Science Source/Getty Images; p. 63 Emin Avundukluoglu/Anadolu Agency/Getty Images; pp. 64–65 Blend Images-Ariel Skelley/Brand X Pictures/Getty Images; interior pages background texture © iStockphoto.com/ Piotr Krzeslak.

CONTENTS

The civil rights movement in the United States underwent a marked shift in emphasis after 1970. The legislative goals of the movement had largely been achieved through the Civil Rights Act of 1964 and the Voting Rights Act of 1965. And even more significant than some of the civil rights laws was President Lyndon Johnson's Great Society program, which encompassed his administration's War on Poverty efforts. One goal of the Great Society was to help realize some of the intentions of civil rights legislation. This could be done only by opening up opportunities for blacks in schooling, housing, and the labor force. Thus, a new emphasis emerged: affirmative action programs in both school admission and job hiring tried to remedy the effects of historical discrimination by assuring present opportunities. These programs helped blacks achieve notable gains in education and allowed black families to rise into the middle and upper middle class, although the use of racial quotas led to later court

Barack Obama—with his wife, Michelle—being sworn in as the 44th president of the United States, on Jan. 20, 2009.

challenges of the policy as a form of "reverse discrimination."

Nevertheless, many blacks continued to face difficult social and economic challenges, especially in the inner cities. A reminder of the lingering tensions in some impoverished city neighborhoods came in 1992, when four white police officers were acquitted in the beating of Rodney King, an African American motorist, in Los Angeles, California. Hours after the acquittal, the city erupted in riots in which more than 50 people were killed. Smaller riots broke out in other U.S. cities.

Meanwhile, African Americans were making big gains in politics in the late 20th and early 21st centuries. The biggest milestone came in 2008, when Barack Obama, a first-term senator from Illinois, became the first African American to be nominated for the presidency by either major party. He went on to challenge Republican senator John McCain for the country's highest office. Obama, bolstered by a fever of popular support, eschewed federal financing of his campaign and raised hundreds of millions of dollars, much of it coming in small donations and over the Internet from a record number of donors. His fund-raising advantage helped him buy massive amounts of television advertising and organize deep grassroots organizations in key battleground states and in states that had voted Republican in previous presidential cycles. Obama won the election, capturing nearly 53 percent of the popular vote and 365 electoral votes. On election night tens of thousands gathered in Chicago's Grant Park to see him claim victory.

Many political observers noted that the election of the nation's first African American president marked a transition into a "post-racial" society. They believed that a black man's rise to the White House meant that racial discrimination was no longer a major concern in American society. In other positive developments, more and more Americans were identifying as multiracial (an increase of 32 percent between 2000 and 2010, according to the U.S. Census). However, severe challenges remained. In the second decade of the 21st century, black Americans continued to lag behind white Americans in income and education and were more likely to be in prison. The shootings of teenagers Trayvon Martin and Michael Brown led to public outcry, just as King's beating had two decades earlier. Incidents such as these suggested that calling America "postracial" might have been dangerously premature.

CHAPTER ONE

BREAKING RACIAL BARRIERS IN THE ARTS, SPORTS, AND ENTERTAINMENT

*I*nvisible Man, Ralph Ellison's novel of alienation and the identity, won the National Book Award for fiction in 1953. Like its nameless, faceless narrator, many blacks in the 1940s searched for identity in a white-dominated society. Their concerns were ignored or neglected. Their accomplishments, except as entertainers, went unrecognized. They were excluded from restaurants, theaters, hotels, and clubs.

In protesting the abuse of human rights, Martin Luther King Jr.'s leadership and the civil rights movement brought high visibility to African Americans. In the era of *Invisible Man*, left-wing causes had exploited them as anonymous symbols of oppression, but the media made celebrities of 1960s activists—for example, Black Panther supporter Angela Davis and Julian Bond of the

Ralph Ellison was an American writer who won distinction with his first novel, *Invisible Man* (1952), which won the 1953 National Book Award for fiction.

Student Nonviolent Coordinating Committee (SNCC), who at age 28 in 1968 was put forward for the Democratic vice presidential nomination. At the forefront of the civil rights marches were author James Baldwin, gospel singer Mahalia Jackson, folksingers Harry Belafonte and Odetta, and comedian Dick Gregory.

The participation of these and other well-known African American artists and performers helped the civil rights movement gain legitimacy during a time when African Americans still faced legal and political barriers because of Jim Crow policies. Even before the civil rights era, however, African Americans had begun to make significant strides toward achieving racial equality in a number of different fields. In the early 20th century, black musicians invented jazz and blues, which had crossover appeal with white listeners. A breakthrough in sports came in 1947 when Jackie Robinson joined the Brooklyn Dodgers. Through advancements such as these, a common culture developed in which the contributions of black Americans were equally valued. Seeing white and black Americans work together in the arts, music, and sports helped change white America's perception of what African Americans could achieve if given equal opportunities. This was a major step in tearing down the barriers created by generations of prejudice and paved the way for blacks to make inroads in politics and other fields as well.

TELEVISION AND FILM

Nat King Cole was the first black entertainer with a network television series (1956–57), but, despite the singer's great talent, his variety show did not attract sponsors. In the decades following Cole's death, in

1965, however, many situation comedies with predominantly black casts were promoted, and the large acting ensembles in dramatic series were often integrated. Redd Foxx and Demond Wilson starred in the popular series *Sanford and Son* from 1972–77. One of the most acclaimed weekly shows ever produced was *The Cosby Show* (1984–92), starring comedian Bill Cosby. Keenen Ivory Wayans, star of the long-running satirical comedy show *In Living Color*, won an Emmy Award for his work in 1990. *The Bernie Mac Show*, a sitcom starring comedian Bernie Mac, won a Peabody Award in 2001.

One of television's most watched dramatic telecasts was *Roots*, an eight-part miniseries first shown in 1977, followed by a sequel, the seven-part *Roots: The Next Generations*, in 1979. Based on author Alex Haley's real-life quest to trace his African ancestry, the series made other African Americans more aware of their rich cultural heritage.

Achievements by African Americans in the field of broadcast journalism included those of Ed Bradley, who became one of the *60 Minutes* interviewers in 1981, and Bryant Gumbel, who became cohost of *The Today Show* in 1982. Charlayne Hunter-Gault appeared regularly on the *MacNeil-Lehrer News Hour.* Jennifer Lawson was a vice president of the Public Broadcasting Service. A former anchor on a local news desk, Oprah Winfrey started a popular daytime talk show in the 1980s. Soon she established her own television and film production companies. Her media entertainment empire made her one of the richest and most influential women in the United States.

In the 1950s Academy Award winner Sidney Poitier appeared in genuine dramatic roles. "Blaxploitation" films like *Superfly* drew huge audiences in the 1970s, but they did not deal with the real black experience. By the 1980s other actors were cast in roles that had not been written specifically for a black person—for example, Louis Gossett Jr. in *An Officer and a Gentleman* (1983 Academy Award). "Buddy pictures" paired black and white actors, including such stars as Eddie Murphy, Danny Glover, Richard Pryor, and Gregory Hines. Hines was also a dazzling tap dancer. In 2002 Halle Berry became the first African American woman to win an Academy Award for best actress, for her role in *Monster's Ball* (2001). Morgan Freeman, Denzel Washington, and Will Smith were among the most popular and acclaimed actors of the early 21st century. A completely original talent, director-writer-actor Spike Lee had total control over his productions, which examined contemporary African American life. Other prominent black directors were John Singleton (*Boyz n the Hood*, 1991) and Matty Rich (*Straight Out of Brooklyn*, 1990).

The film *12 Years a Slave*, based on the true story of Solomon Northup, an American free black man who

Halle Berry starred with Billy Bob Thornton in the movie *Monster's Ball*, becoming the first African American woman to win an Academy Award for best actress.

AFRICAN AMERICAN FILMMAKERS

The emergence of independent African America
ers such as Melvin Van Peebles in the late 196(
1970s paved the way for the mainstream succe
uncompromising black cinema in the late 1980

Writer, director, and ac
Lee is renowned for a
approach to films that
controversial subject n

1990s. The leader of the movement was Spike Lee, an all-around talent who wrote, directed, edited, and often performed in his films. He first demonstrated his confident style in the low-budget comedy *She's Gotta Have It* (1986). Lee's *School Daze* (1988), a satire about class and color at a black college, grossed more than twice its cost. Suddenly, Hollywood saw a market for films with a distinctly African American perspective.

Lee continued his sometimes controversial scrutiny of black life, race relations, and social problems in *Do the Right Thing* (1989), which earned him an Oscar nomination for best screenplay, *Get on the Bus* (1996), and the documentary *Four Little Girls* (1998), among other films. His success provided opportunities for other filmmakers to examine the diversity of the African American experience. At age 23 John Singleton became the youngest filmmaker—and the first African American—to receive a best director Oscar nomination for his work on *Boyz n the Hood* (1991), a powerful depiction of life in south-central Los Angeles. The Hudlin brothers successfully merged teen movies with hip-hop culture in *House Party* (1990). In *To Sleep with Anger* (1990), Charles Burnett documented the disintegration of the middle-class African American family. In 1997 writer-director Kasi Lemmons created an evocative Tennessee Williams–style period piece in *Eve's Bayou*, while *Soul Food*, directed by George Tillman Jr., depicted a proud matriarch and the family she holds together. Tyler Perry created his own empire of African American media in the first two decades of the 21st century. He directed, produced, wrote, and starred in many films and television shows, beginning with 2005's *Diary of a Mad Black Woman*.

was kidnapped and sold into slavery in 1841, won best picture at the 2013 Academy Awards. (The British director, screenwriter, and artist Steve McQueen was nominated for best director and was the first black director to helm an Academy Award best picture winner.) In 2012 actress Kerry Washington of *Scandal* became the first African American woman to star in a drama on network television in almost 40 years. *Black-ish*, a sitcom that debuted in 2014, confronted racial identity and black culture directly, whereas the race of most black characters on television was not treated as an issue.

LITERATURE

The poet Gwendolyn Brooks was the first black author to win a Pulitzer Prize, for *Annie Allen* in 1950. Charles Gordone in 1970 became the first African American playwright to win a Pulitzer, with his depiction of a black hustler-poet in *No Place to Be Somebody*. *The Color Purple*, a best-selling novel by Alice Walker, won a Pulitzer in 1983.

Toni Morrison's novel *Beloved* took the Pulitzer for fiction in 1988, and in 1993 Morrison became the first African American to win the Nobel Prize for Literature. Morrison's later works include *A Mercy* (2008), which deals with slavery in 17th-century America, and *Home* (2012). In 2010 Morrison was made an officer of the French Legion of Honour. Two years later she was awarded the U.S. Presidential Medal of Freedom.

The most accomplished African American dramatist in the second half of the 20th century was August

Gwendolyn Brooks, whose poetry captures the everyday life of urban blacks, became in 1950 the first African American to be awarded the Pulitzer Prize.

Wilson, a two-time Pulitzer Prize winner. Between 1984 and 2005 Wilson chronicled black American life in a series of 10 plays, one set in each decade of the 20th century.

MUSIC

Almost all of America's popular music—including jazz, blues, rock, soul, and hip-hop—has its origins in black culture. Thomas A. Dorsey was the "Father of Gospel Music," and Harry T. Burleigh arranged spirituals for the concert stage. Marian Anderson was the first black artist to sing at the Metropolitan Opera House, in 1955. Other African American opera stars were Leontyne Price, La Julia Rhea, Grace Bumbry, Shirley Verrett, Jessye Norman, and Kathleen Battle. Arthur Mitchell, Alvin Ailey, and Bill T. Jones led outstanding dance troupes. Trumpeter Wynton Marsalis emerged as one of the great trumpeters of the late 20th century, winning Grammy Awards for both jazz and classical works. His brother, Branford, was music director for television's popular *The Tonight Show* from 1992 to 1995.

Top-selling popular recording artists of the late 20th and early 21st centuries included Michael Jackson, Janet Jackson, Prince, Whitney Houston, Mary J. Blige, Beyoncé, Alicia Keys, and Usher. The hip-hop movement, which originated among African Americans in the South Bronx section of New York City in the late 1970s, produced many rap superstars such as 50 Cent, Kanye West, Nas, and Drake. Jay-Z and Pharrell Williams were prominent record producers as well as rappers and singers.

Best-selling musical artist Alicia Keys has won multiple Grammy Awards in addition to her acting and directing work.

SPORTS

The racial barrier in Major League Baseball was broken by Jackie Robinson in 1947. Today African American athletes dominate most of the professional team sports. Some of the many outstanding African American National Basketball Association (NBA) players were Kareem Abdul-Jabbar, Wilt Chamberlain, Magic Johnson, Michael Jordan, Shaquille O'Neal, Kobe Bryant, and LeBron James. In the National Football League (NFL) running backs Walter Payton, Jim Brown, and Emmitt Smith; wide receiver Jerry Rice; defensive end Jim Marshall; and quarterback Russell Wilson set records. Hank Aaron held baseball's career home run record from 1974 until 2007, when he was surpassed by another African American, Barry Bonds. Rickey Henderson broke baseball's stolen-base record in 1991 and set a record for the most career runs scored in 2001. In 2013 the Institute for Diversity and Ethics in Sports reported that 76 percent of NBA players and 66 percent of NFL players were black, compared to only 8 percent of MLB players. However, African Americans were underrepresented as coaches and especially team owners. The only black majority team owner in any of the three major sports leagues was Michael Jordan of the NBA's Charlotte Bobcats.

Since Joe Louis became the heavyweight boxing champion in the 1930s, black Americans have been among the world's top heavyweight fighters. Arthur Ashe, Althea Gibson, Venus Williams, and Serena Williams were at the top of the game of tennis. In 1997 Tiger Woods, the son of an African American father and a Thai mother, became the first golfer of either

Sisters Venus *(left)* and Serena Williams have revolutionized women's tennis, wielding their rackets to deliver some of the strongest serves the game has ever seen.

African American or Asian descent to win the prestigious Masters Tournament.

Since Jesse Owens won four Olympic gold medals in 1936, African Americans have excelled in track and field sports. In 1960 Wilma Rudolph became the first American woman to win three track gold medals in a single Olympics. Florence Griffith Joyner and Jackie Joyner-Kersee won medals at the 1988 Olympics. Carl Lewis, Butch Reynolds, Edwin Moses, Bob Beamon, Michael Johnson, and Gail Devers also set track records. African American medal winners at the 2008 and 2012 Olympics included Angelo Taylor, Walter Dix, Allyson Felix, and Sanya Richards-Ross.

CHAPTER TWO

AFRICAN AMERICANS IN POLITICS AND POSITIONS OF POWER

On the political front, the voter registration drives that intensified during the 1960s began to show results by the end of the decade. In 1960 only about 28 percent of the black voting-age population in the South was registered, and there were perhaps 100 black elected officials. By 1969 with the number of registrants more than doubled, up to 1,185 blacks had been elected to state and local offices. The year 1972 marked the first time that an African American from a major political party, Democrat Shirley Chisholm, ran for her party's nomination for the presidency, though she received less than 3 percent of her party's vote.

On November 4, 2008, by a popular vote of 53 percent to 46 percent and an Electoral College total of 365 to 173 (with 270 needed to win), Barack Obama was elected the 44th president of the United States, making history as the first African American to hold this position. Obama's successful election as president marked the culmination of a long road of political struggles by African American leaders seeking better representation in the political process and equal opportunity to a political voice. The 2014 midterm elections included a record number of African American candidates on the ballots, with more than 100 black candidates in statewide and congressional elections, a trend that has been attributed in part to Obama's historic presidency.

ELECTORAL SUCCESSES

Beginning in the 1960s some of the electoral gains by African Americans were spectacular. The first black chief executive of a major city was an appointee—Walter E. Washington, who became the commissioner of Washington, D.C., in 1967. But other blacks were elected mayor—Carl

Voter registration drives of the 1960s nearly doubled the number of registered African American voters by the end of that decade.

Stokes in Cleveland and Richard Hatcher in Gary, Indiana, in 1967; Kenneth Gibson in Newark in 1969; Tom Bradley in Los Angeles, Coleman A. Young in Detroit, and Maynard Jackson in Atlanta in 1973; Ernest N. Morial in New Orleans in 1977; Richard Arrington in Birmingham in 1979; Wilson Goode in Philadelphia and Harold Washington in Chicago in 1983; and Kurt L. Schmoke in Baltimore in 1987. Also in 1987 Carrie Saxon Perry of Hartford, Connecticut, was the first black woman to be elected mayor of a large city.

An African American became mayor of the largest city in the United States in 1989 when David Dinkins won the general election after a stunning primary defeat of New York City's incumbent mayor. Tom Bradley's attempt to become the country's first elected black governor failed in 1982, but seven years later L. Douglas Wilder of Virginia reached that milestone.

Blacks made gains on the national level as well. The first black senator since the Reconstruction period was Edward W. Brooke of Massachusetts, who served from 1967 to 1979. The first

In 1989 David Dinkins became New York City's first black mayor. Ethnic tensions as well as crime statistics swelled during his term, however, and he was not reelected.

CONDOLEEZZA RICE

U.S. educator and politician Condoleezza Rice (born 1954) was the first woman and the first African American national security adviser in the United States, serving from 2001 to 2005 under President George W. Bush. She became secretary of state in 2005, during Bush's second term. An influential and loyal adviser to Bush, Rice was a strong advocate of the country's so-called war on terrorism and of invading Iraq in 2003. Indeed, many believed she was one of the principal architects of the administration's controversial strategy of acting "preemptively," including using military force, against countries thought to pose a possible threat to the United States.

During the early 1980s Rice conducted research and taught at Stanford University. With a growing reputation as an expert on Soviet-bloc politics, in 1986 Rice became an adviser to the Joint Chiefs of Staff under President Ronald Reagan. During the administration of President George H.W. Bush, she was director and then senior director of Soviet and East European affairs on the National Security Council and a special assistant to the president. Rice returned to Stanford in 1991 and served as its provost from 1993 to 1999.

In 1999 Rice left Stanford to become foreign policy adviser to the presidential campaign of George W. Bush. Upon his becoming president, Bush made her national security adviser. After the terrorist attacks of Sept. 11, 2001, Rice supported the U.S.-led attacks on terrorist and Taliban targets in Afghanistan. She also advocated the overthrow of Iraqi president Saddam Hussein. When the administration drew criticism for the Iraq War, Rice vigorously defended the president's policies.

The first woman and first African American national security adviser (2001–05), Condoleezza Rice was also the first black woman secretary of state (2005–09).

Early in 2005 Rice succeeded Colin Powell as secretary of state. In that post, she brokered negotiations to end Israel's occupation of the Gaza Strip and led the U.S. effort to promote peace between Israel and the Palestinians. She also persuaded North Korea to return to talks in which that country eventually agreed to dismantle its nuclear weapons program. In addition, Rice called for sanctions against Iran after that country did not end its nuclear program or allow inspections of its nuclear facilities. At the end of the Bush presidency in 2009, Rice returned to her academic career at Stanford.

Economist Robert C. Weaver was the Department of the Interior's first African American adviser on racial problems.

African American named to the Supreme Court was Thurgood Marshall, in 1967. When Marshall retired in 1991, another black associate justice, Clarence Thomas, succeeded him.

The first black member of a presidential cabinet was Robert C. Weaver, secretary of Housing and Urban Development (HUD; 1966). Another secretary of HUD, Patricia Roberts Harris, was the first black woman in the cabinet (1977). Andrew Young was named ambassador to the United Nations in 1977. In 1989 Colin Powell, a four-star general in the U.S. Army, was chosen to be chairman of the Joint Chiefs of Staff—the nation's highest military post. In 2001 Powell also became the first African American secretary of state. In 2005 Condoleezza Rice, the first black woman to hold the post, succeeded him as secretary of state.

ASCENT TO THE PRESIDENCY

African Americans reached the pinnacle of U.S. politics when Barack Obama was elected president in 2008. The son of a black father from Kenya and a white mother from Kansas, Obama was a first-term U.S. senator from Illinois when the Democrats selected him as their presidential candidate. His ascent to the presidency was lauded as a great leap forward for race relations in the United States.

Before Obama's rise to the presidency, a number of other prominent African Americans sought high political office. In 1952 the Progressive Party nominated Charlotta A. Bass to be vice president, marking the first time an African American woman had been nominated for that post. In 1968 Shirley Chisholm

Barack Obama's election to the presidency—becoming the first African American president in U.S. history—was acclaimed as a tremendous step in American race relations.

of New York became the first African American woman elected to the House of Representatives, and in 1972 she became the first African American to seek a major party's nomination for the presidency. In 1986 Georgia's 5th Congressional District elected civil rights leader John Lewis to the House of Representatives, and the *Atlanta Journal-Constitution* declared Lewis to be the "only former major civil rights leader who extended his fight for human rights and racial reconciliation to the halls of Congress." And in 1992 Carol Moseley Braun of Illinois became the first African American woman elected to the U.S. Senate.

CHAPTER THREE

BARACK OBAMA

In only four years Barack Obama made an improbable rise from the state legislature of Illinois to the highest office of the United States. The first African American to win the presidency, he made history with his resounding victory in the election of 2008. His eloquent message of hope and change attracted voters across the country, even in states that had gone decades without supporting a Democratic presidential candidate. He was elected to a second term in 2012.

Barack Obama's ascendance to the presidency reflects the hard work and the successes of the civil rights efforts that preceded his campaign. His successful 2008 presidential campaign made history for its record-breaking fund-raising, largely from small donors, as well as its grassroots mobilization of young, poor, and minority voters who had not previously been politically engaged at high rates.

EARLY LIFE AND EDUCATION

Barack Hussein Obama II was born on August 4, 1961, in Honolulu, Hawaii. His father, Barack Obama Sr., was from rural Kenya, and Obama's mother, S. Ann Dunham, came from Kansas. When young Barack was two years old, his parents divorced, and his father eventually returned to Kenya to work as an economist. His mother later married a student from Indonesia.

After high school Obama received a bachelor's degree in political science from Columbia University in 1983. Later he entered Harvard Law School and graduated with honors

The father of the future president—Kenyan Barack Obama Sr., shown here—met and later married the future president's mother, American S. Ann Dunham, while both were college students in Hawaii.

MICHELLE OBAMA

An attorney and university administrator, Michelle Obama is also the wife of Barack Obama, who was elected the 44th president of the United States in 2008. She won many admirers by striking a firm balance between her private family life and her highly public role in her husband's political career.

Michelle LaVaughn Robinson was born on January 17, 1964, in Chicago, Illinois, and grew up on the city's South Side. She earned a bachelor's degree in 1985 and three years later received a degree from Harvard Law School.

When her husband announced his candidacy for the 2008 Democratic presidential nomination, Michelle took a prominent role in his campaign. She took leave from her position at the University of Chicago to devote herself more fully to campaigning while still maintaining time to care for her and Barack's two young daughters. An adept speaker, she stumped extensively for her husband during the long Democratic primary race and then in his general-election campaign against Republican John McCain. Michelle's openness on the campaign trail and in interviews—she often humanized her husband by discussing his faults—endeared her to many. Campaign aides referred to her as "the closer" for her persuasiveness in winning over uncommitted voters who attended rallies. Her efforts contributed to Barack's historic election to the presidency in November 2008.

Michelle Obama was such an effective and persuasive speaker during Barack Obama's campaigns that she was nicknamed "the closer."

in 1991. While working at a Chicago law firm in the summer of 1989, Obama met Chicago native Michelle Robinson, a young lawyer at the firm. The two married in 1992 and had two daughters, Malia and Sasha.

ENTRY INTO POLITICS

After law school Obama returned to Chicago and became active in the Democratic Party. He organized Project Vote, a drive that registered tens of thousands of African Americans to vote. He also practiced civil rights law and taught constitutional law at the University of Chicago.

In 1996 Obama was elected as a Democrat to the Illinois Senate, where he would serve for eight years. As a state senator he helped pass legislation that tightened campaign finance regulations, expanded health care to poor families, and reformed criminal justice and welfare laws. He also served as chairman of the state's Health and Human Services Committee.

In 2004 Obama ran for a seat in the U.S. Senate. In the Democratic primary he emerged as the winner from a field of seven candidates. During the general election campaign Obama's Republican opponent was forced to withdraw after details of his divorce proceedings came to light. The state Republican Party then brought in Alan Keyes, a conservative radio talk-show host and former diplomat who moved to Illinois from Maryland for the contest. It was the first Senate race in which the two leading candidates were African Americans. Obama handily defeated Keyes in November, winning 70 percent of the vote. He was only the third African American to be elected to the Senate since the end of Reconstruction in 1877.

As he campaigned for the Senate, Barack Obama began garnering a lot of attention, particularly after his July 2004 keynote address at the Democratic National Convention.

While campaigning for the Senate, Obama became one of the most talked-about young politicians in a generation. His keynote address at the Democratic National Convention in July 2004 brought conventioneers to their feet and instantly made him a political superstar. The rousing speech wove elements of Obama's biography with the theme that all Americans are connected in ways that transcend political, cultural, and geographical differences. Following the address, Obama's memoir, *Dreams from My Father* (1995), climbed the best-seller lists.

After taking office as a senator in 2005, Obama quickly became a major figure in his party. He received several coveted committee assignments, including a post on the Foreign Relations Committee. He also served on the Environment and Public Works and the Veterans' Affairs committees. He supported ethics reform in government, championed alternative energy sources, and worked to secure or destroy deadly weapons in Russia and elsewhere.

Obama achieved a level of visibility that was rare for a first-term senator. A trip to his father's home in Kenya in August 2006 attracted international

After a close race against the popular senator Hillary Clinton, Obama won his bid for the Democratic presidential nomination.

media attention. His second book, *The Audacity of Hope*, was published weeks later and instantly became a best seller.

NOMINATION AND ELECTION

In early 2007 Obama declared himself in the running for the 2008 Democratic presidential nomination. Obama's personal charisma, stirring oratory, and campaign promise to bring change to the political system won him the support of many Democrats, especially young and minority voters.

On January 3, 2008, Obama won a surprise victory in the first major nominating contest, the Iowa caucus. The primary race that followed was tightly contested. Not until June 3, following the final primaries in Montana and South Dakota, did the number of delegates pledged to Obama surpass the total needed to win the Democratic nomination. Obama officially accepted the nomination at the Democratic National Convention in August, becoming the first African American to be nominated for the presidency by either major party.

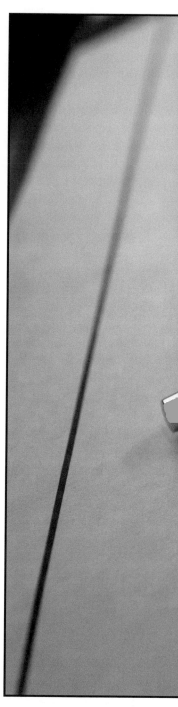

This close-up of Pres. Barack Obama's signature is on the American Recovery and Reinvestment Act.

In November 2008 Obama decisively won the presidency, capturing 365 electoral votes and some 53 percent of the popular vote. A joyous crowd gathered in Chicago's Grant Park to see Obama claim victory on election night. In addition to being the first African American president, he was also the first sitting U.S. senator to win the office since John F. Kennedy in 1960. He was inaugurated president on January 20, 2009.

PRESIDENCY

In his first months in office, Obama worked to restore the international image of the United States, which many believed had been tarnished by the policies of the Bush administration. He ordered the closing of the controversial military detention facility in Guantánamo Bay, Cuba, within a year (a deadline that was not met). He vowed to work toward the elimination of nuclear weapons and to improve strained relations with Russia. In June 2009 he traveled to the Middle East and gave a speech calling for a new relationship between the United States and the Muslim world. In recognition of such efforts, Obama was awarded the 2009 Nobel Peace Prize, with the Nobel Committee citing his "extraordinary efforts to strengthen international diplomacy and cooperation between peoples."

Obama's top domestic priority was the ongoing economic recession. Aided by Democratic majorities in both the Senate and the House of Representatives, Obama pushed a massive stimulus package through Congress, which pumped hundreds of billions of dollars into the struggling economy. By late 2009 the stimulus had reversed the dramatic decline in the gross domestic product. Despite gains, however, unemployment remained high, and Republicans complained that the stimulus had been too costly.

A sweeping financial reform bill passed in July 2010 was another response to the recession. Aimed at preventing the conditions that led to the economic crisis, the bill empowered the government to take over and shut down large troubled financial firms and created a council of federal regulators to monitor the financial system, among other provisions. The passage of the bill was a major legislative victory for the president.

Another early priority of Obama's presidency was reforming the country's health care system. During the election campaign, Obama had called for reforms that would make health insurance more affordable and extend coverage to tens of millions of Americans who lacked it. The issue provoked a prolonged and sometimes bitter debate, with Republicans complaining that Democratic proposals constituted a costly "government takeover" of health care. A new conservative populist movement, the Tea Party, loudly objected to the proposed health care reforms in a series of town hall meetings in summer 2009. More generally, Tea Party members opposed what they saw as excessive taxes and government involvement in the private sector.

In late 2009 the Democrat-controlled House of Representatives and Senate each passed a version of the health care bill. As congressional leaders prepared to negotiate a compromise between the two versions, the triumph of a Republican in a special election held to fill the Senate seat vacated by Ted Kennedy

Stanley McChrystal *(right)* and U.S. Pres. Barack Obama, 2009.

after his death destroyed the Democrats' filibuster-proof majority. In March 2010, as the historic measure teetered on the brink of defeat, Obama and other Democratic leaders mounted a last-ditch campaign to pass it. The president became more forceful in promoting the bill, both to Congress and to the American people. Later that month Congress passed the bill with no Republican support.

Obama's key foreign-policy challenges were the ongoing wars in Iraq and Afghanistan. Throughout the presidential campaign he had argued that the focus of U.S. military efforts should be in Afghanistan rather than Iraq. In keeping with this view, Obama set an 18-month timetable for the withdrawal of U.S. combat troops from Iraq. The situation in Iraq continued to improve, and in August 2010, on schedule, the U.S. combat mission in Iraq ended. The withdrawal of some 50,000 U.S. troops who had remained in the country as a transitional force was completed in December 2011, ending the Iraq War. Meanwhile, after the resurgence of the Taliban in Afghanistan that had begun in 2006, Obama increased the number of U.S. troops there. On May 1, 2011, he announced that U.S. Special Forces had killed Osama bin Laden, leader of the terrorist group al-Qaeda, in a firefight in a compound in Abbottabad, Pakistan.

Elsewhere in the Middle East, popular uprisings brought abrupt ends to longtime authoritarian governments in Tunisia and Egypt and widespread protests and conflict in other countries. The Obama administration voiced its support for the protesters' democratic goals while trying to avoid direct intervention in the affairs of other countries. In Libya, however, Obama felt U.S. intervention was necessary when longtime dictator Muammar al-Qaddafi unleashed a brutal military crackdown on protests against his rule. In March 2011 U.S. and European forces launched air strikes against targets in Libya in an effort to disable that country's air force and air defense systems. A week later the Obama administration relinquished command in Libya to the North Atlantic Treaty Organization.

Obama officially kicked off his bid for reelection in May 2012. His Republican opponent was Mitt Romney, a former governor of Massachusetts. As in 2008 the economy was the central issue of the race. Though economic conditions continued to improve, the recovery was slow and uneven. Romney spent much of his campaign criticizing Obama's handling of the economy, but the Republican's effort fell short.

On November 6, 2012, President Barack Obama won reelection to the presidency, defeating Mitt Romney with 332 electoral votes and was sworn in to office formally on January 21, 2013. While his election was decisive, he would continue to operate in a divided government, with a Democrat-controlled Senate and a Republican-controlled House of Representatives.

The newly reelected president Barack Obama dances with his wife, First Lady Michelle Obama, as they celebrate his victory for a second term.

Among the major pieces of legislation that he signed into law were the No Budget, No Pay Act of 2013, the Violence Against Women Reauthorization Act of 2013, the Bipartisan Student Loan Certainty Act of 2013, and the Gabriella Miller Kids First Research Act of 2014. Marking the 50th anniversary of the Civil Rights Act of 1964, Obama condemned the restrictive voting laws—targeting such issues as photo ID requirements and cuts to early voting—which have disproportionate effects on minorities and the poor. And while the Obama administration faced division within Congress and often-low approval ratings, he was touted as having the best private sector job creation performance in American history, with unemployment claims dropping in 2014 to their lowest rate since 2000.

CHAPTER FOUR

CONTINUED SOCIAL, ECONOMIC, AND POLITICAL INEQUITIES

As Americans of African descent reached each new plateau in their struggle for equality, they reevaluated their identity. The slaveholder labels of *black* and *negro* (Spanish for "black") were offensive, so they chose the euphemism *colored* when they were freed. Capitalized, the label *Negro* became acceptable during the migration to the North for factory jobs. The term *Afro-American* was adopted by civil rights activists to underline pride in their ancestral homeland. But *black*— with its connotations of power and revolution—proved more popular. All these terms are still reflected in the names of dozens of organizations. To reestablish "cultural integrity" in the late 1980s, Jesse Jackson proposed *African American*, which—unlike some "baseless" color label—proclaims kinship with a historical land base. In the early 21st century the terms *black* and *African American* both were widely used.

SEGREGATION

African Americans were legally segregated for a long period of time in the United States, and entrenched social, economic, and political discrimination persisted

American civil rights leader, Baptist minister, and politician Jesse Jackson established the National Rainbow Coalition in 1984, which pursued equal rights for oppressed people, such as African Americans, women, and homosexuals.

after the segregation laws were abolished. From the early 17th to the mid-19th century, large numbers of Africans were brought to the southern United States and enslaved. After the end of Reconstruction, in the late 19th century, the Southern states passed laws requiring the separation of blacks and whites in public facilities and institutions—including transportation, schools, hotels, restaurants, theaters, and other public places. These laws were declared constitutional in 1896 by the Supreme Court in the case *Plessy v. Ferguson*, which allowed for "separate but equal" public facilities. Undoing this segregation was not achieved until after the landmark school desegregation case, *Brown v. Board of Education*, in 1954, which ruled that separate educational facilities were inherently unequal. Later rulings struck down other types of segregation laws, and the Civil Rights Act of 1964 prohibited racial segregation in public accommodations.

In spite of the gains made by African Americans through the civil rights movement, patterns of housing segregation still persist in the cities of the United States. The Fair Housing Act passed by Congress in 1968 made residential segregation a federal offense. But this law applies only when local laws are used to create or maintain segregated neighborhoods. In most cities of the United States, segregation is maintained by factors other than local laws. For example, African Americans who want to buy homes may be steered away from white neighborhoods by real estate agents.

DISPARITIES AND DISCRIMINATION

The burden of overcrowded and substandard housing in the United States is disproportionately greater

DOROTHY HEIGHT

Dorothy Irene Height was born on March 24, 1912, in Richmond, Virginia, but was raised in Rankin, Pennsylvania. She graduated from New York University in the early 1930s with a master's degree in educational psychology. For six decades she dedicated herself to social service. She joined the National Council of Negro Women (NCNW), an organization that comprises civic, church, educational, labor, community,

Dorothy Height, an American civil rights and women's rights activist, was widely respected and used her influence to improve the situations of and provide prospects for African American women.

and professional groups. Height also became involved with the Young Women's Christian Association (YWCA), eventually holding a national office within the organization. In that capacity she was instrumental in helping to desegregate the YWCA facilities. In 1957 she became president of the NCNW, and her accomplishments included organizing voter registration in the South, voter education in the North, and scholarship programs for student civil rights workers. In the 1970s Height helped the NCNW obtain grants to provide vocational training and assist women in opening businesses.

In her later career, Height used her position to call on the black community to make itself more independent. In the 1990s she placed special emphasis on recruiting young people into joining the war against drugs, illiteracy, and unemployment. She also served as a social services expert on local, state, and federal governmental committees concerned with women's issues. Before she retired in 1996, Height helped gain funding for a national headquarters for the NCNW in Washington, D.C., where the organization also housed its Dorothy I. Height Leadership Institute. Throughout the years she won numerous awards, including the Spingarn Medal (1993), Presidential Medal of Freedom (1994), and Congressional Gold Medal (2004). Height died on April 20, 2010, in Washington, D.C.

for nonwhite families than for white families. In 2000 1.1 percent of blacks lived in dwellings lacking complete plumbing facilities, contrasted with 0.4 percent of whites. How crowded or spacious a dwelling is can indicate the quality of housing. In 2000 housing units

George E. C. Hayes, Thurgood Marshall, and James M. Nabrit, Jr. *(from left to right)* celebrate outside the U.S. Supreme Court after the decision in *Brown v. Board of Education of Topeka.*

with a black householder averaged 2.74 persons per housing unit. This compares with 2.43 for housing units with a white householder.

Much of this inferior housing is found in the segregated black neighborhoods of the nation's large cities. Prior to 1948, when the Supreme Court ruled that restrictive covenants, or racial exclusion clauses, in real estate deeds were not enforceable, nonwhites could be legally barred from buying or renting housing in many neighborhoods. Into the 1990s, in a practice known as redlining (as if a red line were drawn around areas), realtors and private sellers prevented minority buyers from seeing houses they were qualified to buy. Although many open-housing laws have been passed, the nation's cities and suburbs remain largely segregated.

One reason for this was the widespread belief among whites that, if black families moved into an all-white neighborhood, property values would fall. Although numerous studies show this belief to be ill founded, it remains a principal basis for segregation. Ironically, "white flight" can be part of a self-fulfilling prophecy as the white families leaving en masse—not the minorities arriving—can adversely affect the housing market.

Residential segregation by race is in part a by-product of segregation by income. Slums and other old districts of the central cities generally contain the oldest and least desirable housing. But it is housing that low-income, largely nonwhite, families can afford, while more affluent, largely white, families can move out to newer and better housing in outlying areas.

Many white families moved to the suburbs to get away from black and other minority families that were moving into inner-city neighborhoods. They expected

Even in the 21st century, compared to whites, far greater numbers of black Americans live in housing with insufficient facilities.

their new suburban communities to remain racially segregated. Racial integration can be effectively discouraged by zoning new residential land at very low densities, for example, by requiring a minimum lot size of as much as 1 acre (0.4 ha) per house. This makes the cost of housing in such areas too high for low-income families, including the great majority of nonwhites. Suburban communities have, in many cases, also barred the construction of subsidized low-cost housing.

Economic and racial segregation in housing has been accompanied by a gradual movement from the cities to the suburbs of manufacturing plants employing large numbers of nonwhite blue-collar workers. Thus more and more of the jobs on which low-income and nonwhite families rely are being moved farther away from the housing available to them.

Nonwhite and other minority families find it more difficult to get mortgage loans because their incomes are generally lower than those of whites. Also, in the past, lending institutions set up credit restrictions based on race. Thus, even minority families with incomes sufficient to meet the necessary mortgage payments could find it difficult to buy a home.

In many U.S. cities, African Americans and immigrant groups are often compelled to live in the oldest and least desirable housing areas, not so much by legal devices as by economic and social pressures.

Despite numerous laws prohibiting racial discrimination, minorities earn less than their white counterparts and distribution of benefits remains unequal. This

disconnect is between what is referred to as *de jure* (by right or law) and *de facto* (in fact) policy. That is, the laws passed have been found not always to be enforced fairly. The state of New York was forced to investigate numerous claims that banks were deliberately cutting off mortgage lending to predominantly minority communities through redlining. This process is in violation of the Fair Housing Act, passed in 1968 with the goal of ensuring equal access to credit. Moreover, while the racial gap in median income has closed slightly since the 1980s, there are still marked differences in earnings, with nonwhite families earning only 65 percent of what white families earned in 2010. Thus, true equality has not yet been achieved in many ways.

VOTING RIGHTS, RACIAL PROFILING, AND POLICE VIOLENCE

The landmark Voting Rights Act of 1965 prevented racial discrimination in voting. States with a history of discriminating against black voters—most of which were in the South—were not allowed to change their election laws unless the Department of Justice approved them. This ensured that the laws did not infringe upon anyone's right to vote or block access to the ballot because of race. But in the 2013 case *Shelby County v. Holder*, the

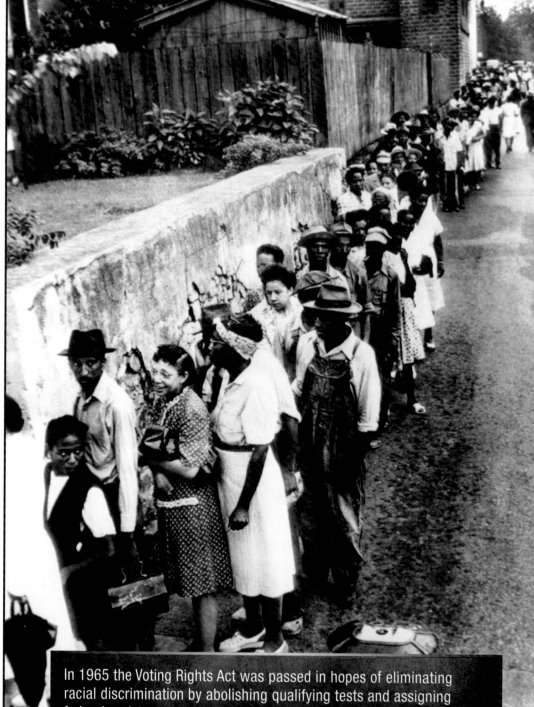

In 1965 the Voting Rights Act was passed in hopes of eliminating racial discrimination by abolishing qualifying tests and assigning federal registrars.

Supreme Court ruled 5–4 that requiring approval based on 40-year-old voter registration and turnout data was unreasonable. In response Texas immediately began to enforce a strict voter identification law. One federal judge estimated that the law could prevent 600,000 voters—mostly poor, black, or Hispanic people, who would be less likely to have an approved photo identification—from exercising their right to vote in 2014. Even so, the Supreme Court allowed the law to stand.

Prejudice against African Americans lingered in other facets of society as well, with sometimes tragic consequences. Trayvon Martin, an unarmed 17-year-old, was killed in Sanford, Florida, on February 26, 2012, by a neighborhood watch volunteer,

The death of Michael Brown reemphasized the need to answer the question of race relations. His killing revived the Twitter hashtag #BlackLivesMatter around the world, including this memorial in Germany.

George Zimmerman, who claimed he acted in self-defense and was acquitted of murder in 2013. The incident sparked protests across the country. President Obama noted, "If I had a son, he'd look like Trayvon," and he acknowledged that Martin's death was part of a much larger social problem in which African American men were treated with suspicion. For example, New York City had a policy known as stop and frisk, in which police officers questioned citizens and checked them for weapons. Between 2004 and 2012 only 12 percent of people stopped were actually arrested or ordered to appear in court. Worse, 83 percent of people affected were African American or Latino. Against growing outrage that the polisy discriminated against minorities, the New York Police Department began to phase out stop and frisk at the end of 2013.

On August 9, 2014, another fatal shooting of an unarmed black teenager incited controversy about racial relations in the United States. Michael Brown was shot by a white police officer, Darren Wilson, in Ferguson, Missouri, a suburb of St. Louis. Though 67 percent of Ferguson's population was black, only 6 percent of its police

Because their incomes are often much lower than whites, nonwhites and other minorities may not have an easy time procuring mortgages for suitable housing.

officers were black. In the following days, thousands of people protested in the streets, mostly peacefully but with some looting and rioting. The St. Louis County Police reacted with tear gas, smoke bombs, and other extreme tactics. The militarization of that police department, as well as others in the country, was widely criticized. The governor of Missouri eventually deployed the National Guard to restore peace in the area.

In yet another high-profile incident of aggressive police mindset, an unarmed black man named Eric Garner died on July 17, 2014, in Staten Island, New York, after arresting officer Daniel Pantaleo put him in a chokehold, a tactic barred by the New York Police Department. In both the Michael Brown and Eric Garner cases, the police officers involved were not indicted. In March 2015, however, the U.S. Department of Justice, while clearing Darren Wilson of civil rights violations, released a scathing report that concluded that the police force in Ferguson had engaged in systemic discrimination and unconstitutional practices against the city's African American residents.

Brown's shooting and the civil unrest that followed raised difficult questions about race in America. According to the Pew Research Center, black and white Americans had very different reactions to the incident. Among those surveyed 80 percent of blacks agreed that it "raises important questions about race," compared to only 37 percent of whites. In fact more whites (47 percent) believed that "race is getting more attention than it deserves."

CONCLUSION

In 2010 there were about 42 million Americans with African roots. They made up about 13 percent of the total U.S. population. One-quarter of African Americans lived in poverty, and discrimination against African Americans remains a problem today. Nevertheless, African Americans have made great gains since the end of slavery more than 150 years ago.

A number of landmark changes have been made that have enhanced the representation and opportunities of minorities in the United States. In 2012 Americans elected a record number of minorities to Congress, with 74 minorities elected and the House Democrats being the first caucus in U.S. history not to have a white male majority. Yet recent events (for example, the fatal police shooting of Michael Brown and the aftermath in Ferguson, Missouri) demonstrate the persistence of racial tensions and the vast progress that remains to be made. While America appears to be far from postracial—indeed, much of American history has been defined by issues surrounding race—what the recent decades' developments may have permitted is a more constructive dialogue about how to address the nation's systemic racial tensions and make continued social progress moving forward.

TIMELINE

1947

Jackie Robinson becomes the first African American athlete to play in baseball's major leagues in the 20th century.

1950

Poet Gwendolyn Brooks becomes the first black author to win a Pulitzer Prize, for *Annie Allen.*

1953

Ralph Ellison's novel *Invisible Man* wins the National Book Award.

1955

Marian Anderson becomes the first black artist to sing at the Metropolitan Opera House.

1961

Barack Hussein Obama II is born in Honolulu, Hawaii.

1967

Walter E. Washington becomes the commissioner of Washington, D.C. He is the first black chief executive of a major city.

1968

Julian Bond becomes the first black man to have his name placed in nomination for the vice presidential candidacy of a major party.

Martin Luther King, Jr., is assassinated on April 4.

1977

The eight-part television series *Roots* airs.

1984

Wynton Marsalis is the first musician to have won Grammy Awards for both classical and jazz recordings.

1989

L. Douglas Wilder is elected governor of Virginia.

1990

David Dinkins becomes mayor of New York City.

Director Spike Lee's screenplay for *Do the Right Thing* is nominated for an Oscar.

1991

African American Rodney King is brutally beaten on March 3 by four white police officers after a high-speed car chase through Los Angeles, California.

1992

Riots break out in Los Angeles after officers are acquitted by a jury on April 29 of charges in the beating of Rodney King.

1997

Michael Jackson is inducted into the Rock and Roll Hall of Fame as a member of the Jackson 5.

2001

Condoleezza Rice becomes the first woman and the first African American national security adviser in the United States.

Michael Jackson is inducted into the Rock and Roll Hall of Fame as a solo performer.

2002

Halle Berry becomes the first African American to win an Academy Award for best actress.

2008

Barack Obama becomes the first African American to be nominated for the presidency on August 27.

2009

Obama is inaugurated as U.S. president on January 20.

Obama is awarded the Nobel Peace Prize.

2012

On November 6 Obama is reelected to a second term as president.

GLOSSARY

ADEPT Highly skilled or well-trained.

AFFIRMATIVE ACTION An active effort to improve employment or educational opportunities for members of minority groups and women.

ALIENATION A withdrawing or separation of a person or a person's affection from an object of past attachment.

AUTHORITARIAN Expecting strict obedience to one's authority.

BIPARTISAN Representing or composed of members of two parties; specifically marked by or involving accord and cooperation between two major political parties.

BLAXPLOITATION The exploitation of blacks by producers of black-oriented films.

CAUCUS A closed meeting of members of a political party or faction usually to select candidates or decide policy.

CHRONICLED Presented a record of in, or as if in, a chronicle.

COVENANTS Solemn agreements.

DESEGREGATE To rid of segregation.

DIPLOMACY The work of keeping up relations between the governments of different countries.

ELOQUENT Having or showing clear and forceful expression.

ESCHEWED Shunned or avoided.

EUPHEMISM A polite, tactful, or less explicit term used to avoid the direct naming of an unpleasant, painful, or frightening reality.

GRASSROOTS Being, originating, or operating in or at the basic or local level of society.

INCUMBENT The holder of an office or position.

INEQUITIES Instances of injustice or unfairness.

INTEGRATION Acceptance as equals into society of persons of different groups (as races).

JIM CROW Discrimination (as in educational opportunity, social rights, or transportation facilities) against a racial or ethnic group other than white and especially against blacks in the Southern U.S. by either legal enforcement or traditional sanctions and usually by restrictive measures designed to prevent intermingling (as of blacks with whites) on equal terms in public places.

KEYNOTE ADDRESS An address (as at a political convention) intended to present the issues of primary interest to the assembly but often concentrated upon arousing unity and enthusiasm.

KINSHIP The quality or state of being kin.

ORATORY The art of speaking in public eloquently or effectively.

POPULIST A member of a political party purporting to represent the rank and file of the people.

PREEMPTIVELY Before others can do so (as in acting before others can do so).

PROVOST A person appointed to superintend, preside over, or be the official head of an institution or corporate body.

QUOTA A share or part assigned to each member of a group.

REGISTRARS An official recorder or keeper of records.

RESURGENCE A rising again into life, activity, or notice.

SANCTIONS Formal decrees.

SATIRICAL Meant to make fun of and show the weaknesses of human nature or a particular person.

SEGREGATION The separation or isolation of a race, class, or group (as by restriction to an area or by separate schools).

STUMPED Went about making political speeches.

TALIBAN A fundamentalist Islamic militant group in Afghanistan.

Black Immigration Network

c/o Black Alliance for Just Immigration

1212 Broadway

Oakland, CA 94612

(917) 310-3785

Website: http://blackimmigration.net

The Black Immigration Network (BIN) is a national network focused on supporting the economic and social policies that help the communities of African Americans and black immigrants "achieve social, economic, and political power." Its ultimate goal is "to create a more just and equitable society."

Black Organizing Project

1035 W Grand Avenue

Oakland, CA 94607

(510) 891-1219

Website: http://blackorganizingproject.org/

The Black Organizing project organizes and builds communities with the goal of creating racial, social, and economic justice.

British Columbia Black History Awareness Society (BCBHAS)

216 Michigan Street

Victoria, BC V8V 1R3

Canada

Website: http://www.islandnet.com/~bcbhas/index.html

The British Columbia Black History Awareness Society (BCBHAS) was created in 1994 to heighten awareness of the history and contributions of blacks in British Columbia.

International Human Rights Association of American Minorities (IHRAAM)

101 - 5170 Dunster Road, Suite 117

Nanaimo, BC V9T 6M4

Canada

IHRAAM-USA

332 South Michigan Avenue, Suite 1032-I235

Chicago, IL 60604-4434

Website: http://www.ihraam.org/AfricanAmericanProject.html

The International Human Rights Association of American Minorities (IHRAAM) enables and synchronizes the efforts of national minorities, indigenous peoples, and unrepresented and occupied peoples and nations to gain access to international law and its enforcement mechanisms concerning human rights and the right to self-determination.

National Association for the Advancement of Colored People (NAACP)

National Headquarters

4805 Mt. Hope Drive

Baltimore MD 21215

Toll-Free: (877) NAACP-98

Website: http://www.naacp.org

Since 1909 the National Association for the Advancement of Colored People (NAACP) has been advocating for rights for all, as well as striving to eliminate discrimination based on race.

National Coalition of 100 Black Women

1925 Adam C. Powell Jr. Boulevard

Suite 1L

New York, NY 10026

(212) 222-5660

Website: http://www.ncbw.org

The National Coalition of 100 Black Women is a nonprofit, volunteer-run organization that supports all women and strives for racial and gender equality.

National Council of Negro Women, Inc.

633 Pennsylvania Avenue NW

Washington, DC 20004

(202) 737-0120

Website: http://www.ncnw.org

Founded in 1935, the National Council of Negro Women, Inc., leads, educates, and supports women of African descent in their efforts to support their communities and families with services and programs within their communities in the United States and Africa.

National Urban League

120 Wall Street

New York, NY 10005

(212) 558-5300

Website: http://nul.iamempowered.com

The National Urban League supports a movement to empower African Americans in economic independence, equality, influence, and civil rights.

Southern Poverty Law Center

400 Washington Avenue

Montgomery, AL 36104

(334) 956-8200 or Toll-Free at (888) 414-7752

Website: http://www.splcenter.org

The Southern Poverty Law Center is dedicated to fighting hate and bigotry and to seeking justice for the most vulnerable members of our society. Founded by prominent civil rights lawyers in 1971, its goal is to ensure that the promises of the civil rights movement are maintained.

WEBSITES

Because of the changing nature of Internet links, Rosen Publishing has developed an online list of websites related to the subject of this book. This site is updated regularly. Please use this link to access the list:

http://www.rosenlinks.com/AAE/Obama

BIBLIOGRAPHY

Abramson, Jill. *Obama: The Historic Journey*. New York, NY: Callaway Editions, 2009.

Bell, G. S. *In the Black: A History of African Americans on Wall Street*. Hoboken, NJ: Wiley, 2002.

Bloom, Harold. *August Wilson*. New York, NY: Chelsea House, 2009.

Bower, A. L., ed. *African American Foodways: Explorations of History and Culture*. Champaign, IL: University of Illinois Press, 2009.

Chang, Jeff. *Can't Stop, Won't Stop: A History of the Hip-Hop Generation*. New York, NY: St. Martin's Press, 2013.

Daley, James, ed. *Great Speeches by African Americans*. Mineola, NY: Dover Publications, 2006.

Elam, H. J., Jr., and David Krasner, editors. *African-American Performance and Theater History*. New York, NY: Oxford University Press, 2001.

Glass, B. S. *African American Dance*. Jefferson, NC: McFarland, 2007.

Hansen, Joyce. *Women of Hope: African Americans Who Made a Difference*. New York, NY: Scholastic, 2007.

Hine, Darlene Clark, William C. Hine, and Stanley C. Harrold. *African Americans: A Concise History*. 3rd ed. Upper Saddle River, NJ: Prentice Hall, 2009.

Lewis, Samella. *African American Art and Artists*. 3rd ed. Oakland, CA: University of California Press, 2003.

Obama, Barack. *The Audacity of Hope*. New York, NY: Crown, 2013.

Obama, Barack. *Dreams of my Father*. New York, NY: Crown, 2010.

Peretti, B. W. *Lift Every Voice: The History of African American Music*. Lanham, MD: Rowman & Littlefield, 2009.

Robinson, Tom. *Barack Obama: 44th U.S. President*. Edina, MN: ABDO, 2009.

Samuels, W. D. *Encyclopedia of African-American Literature.* New York, NY: Facts on File, 2007.

Schuman, Michael. *Barack Obama: "We Are One People."* Rev. and exp. ed. Berkeley Heights, NJ: Enslow, 2009.

Wagner, Heather Lehr. *Barack Obama.* New York, NY: Chelsea House, 2008.

Wallenfeldt, Jeffrey H. *The Black Experience in America: From Civil Rights to the Present.* New York, NY: Britannica Educational Pub., 2011

Wiggins, D. K., ed. *Out of the Shadows: A Biographical History of African American Athletes.* Fayetteville, AR: University of Arkansas Press, 2006.

INDEX

T

V

W